HOORAY FOR LOVE

Hooray for Love!
a lyrical journey to the source

FRANK CROCITTO

CANDLEPOWER

CANDLEPOWER
New Paltz, NY

copyright 2002 by Frank Crocitto

FIRST EDITION

Crocitto, Frank
Hooray for Love! : a lyrical journey to the source /
Frank Crocitto. -- 1st ed.
      p. cm.
 ISBN 0-9677558-6-7 -- ISBN 0-9677558-7-5 (pbk.)
1. Love--Literary collections. 2. Love in literature. I. Title.
PS3603.R63 H66 2002
818'. 609--dc21

                              2001007851

www.candlepower.org

To My Beloved

Betty

SELECTIONS

She
a poetic revelation

May I in the Merry Merry
a tale of unexpected love

When a Lady Stands Up
an episode of self-possession

My Wife, My Life
an unabashed confession

Autumn Love
a vignette of ripeness on the vine

O Fathomless Love
a drama underseas

Hooray for Love
notes on the only thing
worth doing

Love

was
the subject
of song long before
it became the subject
of poems, and it was the subject
of poems before it became the subject of books,
and now that it is the subject of books,
it is the subject of more and more books.

Which is all well and good
except why must *it*—it being love—
be subject, when by all rights it should be object.

Something subject is below,
subservient, an occasion or vehicle for something else,
like a song, a poem, a book.

Love should not be subject to anything.

Love

is

the object,
the thing to aim for,
the desirable thing.
A song, poem or book should serve *it*.

So here then is a book with love as its object.

Granted, not your everyday book.
More a pleasure boat
woven of vines and flowers—prose and poems.
Something to sail in, to cruise in, to run the rapids in too,
through young love, ripe love, married love,
love of-and-through
all life
arriving, ultimately,
at an unexpected shore.

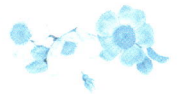

She

to the heart's harbor

When
the truth that lives
in the heart breaks free it
takes wing on words of sweet
simplicity. In this modest poem, a lover,
gazing upon his beloved,
is drawn deeper into
the warmth of
love.

SHE

She's with her grandson
in the meadow
now,
laughing with him,
blowing the heads off
dandelions,
snatching monarchs
in the high grass.

She's grey-haired now,
secure and ripe,
spinning in her balanced
beauty
like a gyroscope set
in the glowing
of an Indian summer sun.

Gently, without
making much of it,
she is hauling me,

HOORAY

full-cargoed
into the harbor
of her heart.
See, her hands are my hands,
her hopes,
her pain even,
her penmanship, too,
is mine.
I've watched her grow
more gorgeous with
each new loop
of the moon.
I've held her night after night
as sleep slowly saturates her.
I've felt her warmth,
her breathing and the sudden
twitch
that precedes her going to
wherever she goes.
And I have,

SHE

in those lingering hours,
drifted in regret
that I haven't known
her in all her phases.

Now her daughter-in-law
has arrived
to take her little boy
away.

Just yesterday
she left me a note
saying how she loved me
and that she is me.
And though
I know it to be so,
I also know
that if it wasn't true,
I would have wanted her
to write it anyway—
I would have wanted
to receive it anyway.

HOORAY

And now up
from the meadow
she comes,
gold earrings glittering
eyes sparkling
full of smiles
as if she's carrying an armful of
fruit.

And now she's holding me
and gazing
up into my eyes
as if I was
the mountain of God.

And I tell her
how lucky I am
but she will hear
none of it.

I insist,
but she only laughs.

Just like I laugh.

*May I
in the
   Merry Merry*

a tale of fresh love

So,
we are brought
together, God knows how,
from God knows where, to a
meeting place where sparks can arc,
heart to heart. The two meeting here
are unlikely lovers, in an unlikely
place, in the highly
likely month of
May.

MAY I IN THE MERRY MERRY

*A*h when spring comes a-tiptoeing onto the isle of *Manahatta* how the songbirds do tweet, how the pigeons do bravely strut. How the brash sea-breeze drives in to dally with the fragrance of new grass and sweet blooms springing from the heart of flowering things. And how this park, on the Island's south end, once the scene of revolutionary ardor and clash of hostile wills, stirs with the unimaginable hopes of yet another spring.

This petite park, this pad of green, this place of peace, at the confluence of two grand rivers, sequestered from the asphalted, concreted, girdered, glassed and mortared madness of the town, is to the mind of a certain young lady, the ideal spot—as long as the weather holds and the sky stays blue—a perfect place to lounge upon a park bench and read away the hours.

To this purpose a chauffeur has whisked her down the FDR Drive before her mother wakes with a better idea of what a well-placed young lady should be doing with her time. This wily Miss Holloway, this Regina Holloway believes spring is calling us to the great outdoors, not to the great indoors of New York department stores. With her college symposia behind—for a week—and the solicitations of dear, simple Harry Hopper, her worshiper and mascot, what a relief it is for her to be home, under the sun, on her blessed island, to loaf in the onrush of spring.

So Regina reads and breathes and

breathes and reads. Now and again, lifting her languorous hazel eyes off the grip of the printed page, she checks for soot that falls in flakes on her pink suit, she scans the expansive green and the sunlit harbor. Whether due to the narcotic of the new season or her well-oiled habit of some years she slides all too easily into dreams and—from no discernible cause—awakens, then wonders where she has been and goes back to her book.

Life in the little park winds along inscrutable paths. On the east side two picturesque old men with canes, dragging their feet, drift towards the seawall. Their common subject so agitates them it stirs them enough to set them shouting and to a clashing of canes. A tot in a sailor suit leaves his guardian to more minutely observe the old men's antics. To the west a bouncy, bosomy mammy decked in white taffeta steers a double-seated stroller along a bumpy winding path—too hastily for the wailing babes within it— heading for the man with hair slicked back who waits beneath the sycamore.

Amidst these wayward pleasure-paths industry pursues its relentless course. A bald member of the tribe of parkees, in a stained green uniform, toils wearily from bench to bench, bearing his dripping brush and bucket of green paint. The parkee's shoulders are round, his head hangs downward. His eyes have the dull look of civil servants doomed to watch a clock that ticks with agonizing slowness.

Once he completes the greening of the rails, none too neatly, he props up a wet-paint sign upon them, heedless of the zephyr that yearns to blow it off or flip its face down. Careless as he is—care-free, as he would maintain—he clings doggedly to an occupation that holds neither sufficient pay nor satisfaction, trusting his imminent retirement will bring him both.

Chic and bored Regina Holloway, on her yet-to-be-painted bench, keeps a drowsy eye upon the parkee's progress. She estimates that at his present speed he will not assault her bench till well after lunchtime. She yawns and lets her book close. She is tired of the mental gyrations of John Donne anyway. A sentence forms in her mind:

> *Poems of sensuous wit and witty sensuality
> do indeed leave something to be desired.*

Ho-hum. A good one to insert in her term paper. Something clever should be said about his religious poems but she has run out of inspiration. Why had he donned the cloth? He was so much more appealing as Wild Jack.

Her mind grazed over the inutility of collegiate themes, of college as a way of life—one her mother has groomed her for—and stopped its chewing just short of *all* human endeavor. Reminding herself that she is barely twenty-one with her whole loaf ahead of her, as mother says, does not ameliorate her stew of discontent.

Here cometh Vincent J. Sciaputo, a young man who labors but a block away, searching for a peaceful place to eat his humble lunch.

HOORAY

The morning has been awful; the afternoon promises to be worse. Lunch may be his only gratification of the day. The room he moils in with twelve other galley slaves, each chained to a cubicle, has not a blessed window, and the conditioned air that bluffles through it smells like a dying sofa. After going through five jobs in six months, his father's ultimatum haunts his hours.

—You lose this one and you're out on the street, dumbo.

A good lunch hour will get him through the day. He carries his good lunch in a paper bag. Ho! Vincent J. is deadset to weather whatever storms heave the deck of KEEN BROTHERS MUNICIPAL BONDS' ship.

He moves energetically from bench to bench, with increasing frustration. He speculates eating on the grass, but he remembers how hard it is to get grass stains off a powder-blue suit. He is sweating now. He removes his jacket—throws it over his shoulder—he rolls up his cuffs—he loosens his tie and tosses it cavalierly over his other shoulder.

—Where the hell do you sit around here? he grumbles at the parkee. You had all winter to paint.

—Can't paint in the winter.

—You do *anything* in the winter?

Like a sphinx the parkee points to the last unpainted bench, then brings his nose back to his task.

—T'anks. When I got up this morning I knew it was gonna be a great day. Hubba hubba.

Today Vinnie is not in the mood for pink. Ordinarily, it being his favorite color and having always been so, he would have been elated by the sight of it, especially when wrapped so stylishly about the human form. Not today. Perhaps, as he has theorized, it was the first color his eyes fell upon, the pink of his mother's blouse. Or as his brother Philly—the Earth Science teacher—snidely suggests, it might have been the pink of the insides of his eyelids that he saw first. Regardless of the attraction of pink, this is the day he has vowed to resist its usual power over him.

One glance did it. Her casual, defiant slouch—he didn't like it. And he didn't like the way she stretched her long legs out and put the heel of one foot on the toe of the other. Plus the way she loafed there, reading, as if there was nobody else in the world. An uptown snob if there ever was one.

He had her pigeon-holed to perfection. As a sworn enemy of affectation, a deep despiser of snobs, Vinnie took her existence as a personal affront. That she dared to wear pink only poured more hot sesame oil on his soul.

Though he appeared self-composed, Regina's silken pink worked on Vinnie like red does on a bull. Always ready to take a dare, he was daring himself to eat his way through his lunch without uttering a word to the other occupant of the bench. Here was a happy conjunction of method and matter: Vinnie's strategy for calming emotional agitation was to eat on.

So Vinnie ate, Regina read—each to the smoldering annoyance of the other. Time trickled by. Perhaps sixty or seventy seconds. By then, having long forgotten his self-inflicted dare, Vinnie found himself absorbed by the notion that only a cad would sit eating in front of a person and not offer them a single morselette.

—Things are really poppin' up green around here, he burst out. Ain't they? You notice?

The lady in pink nodded a frosty assent and continued reading. Her unbridled mind rushed to judgment on his words:

-Not the usual platitude.

-Not profound.

-At least not rehearsed.

-Not as atrocious as expected.

-Pleasant voice.

-Lousy grammar.

"Ain't" always made her wince—Brooklyn or the Bronx, she surmised. Then and there, she decided that her day was ruined. She would leave in a moment and go bury herself in a movie.

—Gets me that they gotta paint the benches right at lunchtime, he went on valiantly. People need to eat. Y'know what I mean?

Once again she nodded, without turning her head.

—Looks like we got the only one undone. Sort of makes us fortune's favorites.

Not even Vinnie knew where he got "fortune's favorites." But it sounded impressive enough for a smile to break in the pit of his belly.

"Undone" was the word that caught Regina. Had he seen the cover of her book? Was he punning on John Donne's name like Donne himself had done? He had given it such a lilt of significance. Maybe he's not as stupid as he looks. Of course, she had not gotten a very good look at him. At his approach, she had moved no muscles other than the ones that control the side-shifting of the eyes.

—D'ya like salami? Vinnie queried her, chewing flamboyantly.

—Excuse *me*?! Ah! The words were out—her head had turned—she was in the game!

—I happen to have a salami sandwich here. I see you got no lunch so I'm offering you half. Good salami. Nothing wrong with it. Great salami! My mother made the hero, too.

I'll bet she did, Regina said to herself as she gnashed her teeth. A tidal wave of perversity swamped the so-sophisticated soul of Regina Holloway. She longed to ask for it *all*. Not half. All, all, all, in a fiendish wolfish howl! To fling it all on the ground and grind it under her heel and lecture him on the necessity of detached and whole-hearted giving.

—That's very kind of you, she replied with extra sugar in her politeness. At least, she congratulated herself, she was being true to her upbringing.

—D'zat mean no? Vinnie prodded. Or could it mean yesss?!

—Yes, it means no!

—Then no may mean yes! he crowed. Oh ho, when we turn the words around we turn the world around! Right or wrong?

Regina turned away, sighing a long world-weary sigh and curled, swan-like, over her *John Donne*. She hoped body language spoke with more finality than words.

—Now, if you don't mind me saying so, there's no sense being bashful. It's good salami, too. It's *kosher*. I don't offer it to everybody.

Regina retorted in a flash.

—I'm not Jewish!! So it doesn't matter!!

Undaunted, his mouth bulging with his Italian hero, Vinnie leapt to his feet jubilantly.

—That's great! Neither am I! So we got something in common after all.

He did a quick jig, a spin and bowed like

a courtier before her.

    Hiding a smile, she muttered into her palm.

—Common, yes, common.

She said it as if she had a mouth full of chokecherries. She gave him her back.

Though Regina had drawn the curtain and was boring intently through the labyrinthine mind of John Donne, Vinnie watched her through the corner of a gleaming eye. He craned his neck and detected an uncontrolled twitching at the corner of her mouth. He knew she wasn't reading, she was going over in her mind what had just transpired. He had amused her. He foresaw the beginnings of a victory. She was conceited and she was contemptuous, yet something in her hazel eyes had lit a candle inside his hairy chest.

—Look, Mister Charming, Regina exploded—or whatever your name is—I know I'm expected to take all this attention and salami as a compliment. But I do not. I came here to read and to be alone. I can assure you I have not the least yearning to be picked up! And if I did it would certainly—

—Picked up?! Vinnie was aghast. Is that what this had been about? I'm very sorry, then. You certainly know how to use a dagger.

—Please, don't attempt to play on my sympathy. I wouldn't mind if you had showed some class, some semblance of style. But to offer me a salami sandwich! Really!

To Regina's surprise Vinnie was visibly hurt. He wiped his mouth with his napkin and turned away. Sullenly, he threw some crumbs to the pigeons.

—If I had wished to speak with you, she continued a little more gently, believe me, I would have spoken, but I have no wish to speak so I am not speaking.

Though offended even more by this condescension, he resolved to leave all hurt behind. He put on a bright face and returned to the joust.

—Well give me a crown and call me Sheba! You must be part of the royal aristocracy. 'If I had a wish to speak I would have spoken.' Well, I tell you what I will do—I shall speak to these here pigeons. Perhaps they shall appreciate me.

—Please do, she said hotly, stung by his mockery. Maybe you'll have an even exchange of ideas!

This last jab tickled Vinnie, so—with unexpected style—he proceeded to deliver a philippic to the pigeons, emphasizing the human race's general frigidity of heart.

Vincent J.'s performance was inspired, a triumph. His realization that the lady in pink was more than an uptown snob, and more than a pretty face, had kindled his imagination. She was a *woman*. A woman who knew her own mind. A woman with spunk—a rare quality, an admirable quality, a queenly quality!

Despite Regina's wall of concentration,

Donne's poetics could not hold a candle to Mr. Vincent Sciaputo's speech to the pigeons. She could resist no longer. She closed the book. And with new-found admiration she inquired why he would not let her be.

—Because I'm going to marry you, he answered.

—Is that a fact? She laughed expansively.

—It is. A very exact fact.

—Might I have something to say about it? Just a little something?

—You might, if you want.

—I do want. I think it's the most absurd thing I've ever heard. And you are the most absurd person. I don't even know you. And, fortunately, you don't know me!

—All the more reason to get to know one another. Lifted on an inspired glimpse into the future, Vinnie begins to dance with an imaginary bride, humming all the while a tune that sounds very much like "Getting To Know You."

—And, she cut in, I'm happy to say, I don't even *like* you.

—I don't like you either, but that's the best basis for a marriage of love.

—Dear God, you're impossible. What is your name?

—Vinnie Sciaputo—from Bay Ridge! And yours?

—Regina Holloway—from Chelsea!

—Well, now it's official, he giggled.

—Bay Ridge. Then the accent's *Brooklyn*—not the Bronx!

—Me got no accent, Kemosabe.

—Nooo, of course you don't.

—Well, the truth is everybody's got some kinda accent. Ain't that so? Mine's Brooklynese. I speak *perfect* Brooklynese. It's the source of my charm.

That he was exasperating was indisputable; ridiculous as well. Certainly too short, and his nose drooped over a little too much.

Besides, he was nerve-wracking; he moved like a wildcat in a cage. You never knew what he was going to do or say. He was always pushing things further than they should go and certainly never knew when to stop. All good reasons among an ever-growing list of reasons to keep him at bay. Still, he was amusing, no doubt of that, and since he had invaded her bench she found herself refreshingly free of her usual boredom. He was as pungent and open-faced as his salami sandwich.

    Lacking the debatable benefits of a college education, Vinnie was forced to rely on his innate resourcefulness of mind. So, with a witty remark here and a pertinent observation there, he managed to engage the high and mightily cultivated Regina in a conversation that ranged from what triggers sap rising in the trees to the pros-and-cons of free will and predestination to imponderables regarding the peculiar way fate has of tossing odd types together, to whether there are such things as types, to the enigmatic character of Wild Jack Donne and how very, very close sex is to religion. And finally to one of Vincent J.'s favorite topics—feet.

Many a fine thing had transpired—some flagrant, some subtle—during that fair day's lunch hour on that fated and unpainted bench. One of the least notable and most noticeable was how Regina, yielding to an old nervous habit, slipped off her shoes, wriggled her toes and rubbed her feet together like a fly. Though he had an abundance of sights and sounds to occupy him, Vinnie could not miss this one. The sight of her feet bare in the unbounded sunshine struck a chord of rapture in his soul.

—You know, Regina, you have absolutely gorgeous feet.

—How very kind of you to say so, she warbled uneasily.

—You have the most beautiful feet that I have ever seen—if you don't mind me saying so. I ain't kidding either. I am an aficionado of feet. I know plenty of girls and their feet. Most of their feet are all squashed and squeezed together with bumps and corns and bulging bunions. That's because of the shoes they wear, I know. But it makes their feet hard to look at. They may have a nice sweet face but what good is it if the feet are ugly? People don't focus on feet enough. Feet are the last frontier. Beautiful feet—feet that don't stink either—are a pleasure to be around. You understand I'm not talking about fetishy stuff. Beauty, I'm talking about beauty. Like, did you ever hear of that sculptor Rodin—he knew about feet. Maybe me and him are the only ones who really know. Ever really look at a foot? There's a true beauty to a foot. It almost sums up the whole beauty of a person.

As Vinnie rolled on, Regina began to imagine how fiendishly exhilarating it would be to bring him home to mother, or to show him off to her friends, including Harry Hopper. Harry, who she'd had hanging about her for ten years, was, she had to admit, a poor excuse for a boyfriend. His trust fund was chock full but all the rest of him was empty. Even the way Vinnie mispronounced Rodin had a certain dash to it, which made her refrain from correcting him.

—Sometimes when I first get to know a girl, Vinnie continued, I drop in on them by surprise. Purposely—because girls like to go around their house in bare feet. I gotta get my sights on them. Of course, I don't have to do that with you. And if their feet are nice, you know, and smooth like marble and clean with that classical shape I can't resist, they got me. I fall all over them. Yours, Regina, yours are like a queen's.

The parkee, freshly back from Mario's Pizza Paradise, with his brush and can in hand, trudged toward the last of his unpainted benches. He stopped and scratched his head. He was as perplexed as Maimonides to see the wiseguy in the powder-blue suit kneeling before the chick in pink and, yes, in broad daylight, kissing her feet.

—Stop it, you lunatic, Regina whizz-purred desperately. Yet she was flattered and most pleasantly embarrassed.

—What've we got to hide? Vinnie declared, looking up. There's nobody around. He had a firm grip on her wriggling feet.

—That man is looking right at us!

—Him? He works for the park. He's seen everything.

—I am not going to allow you to kiss my feet—anymore! Vinnie, do you hear?

—One more, just once more.

—Vincent, will you please get up off your knees. You're going to ruin your suit.

Vinnie did get up, reluctantly. And the girl and boy did, eventually, surrender their bench to the industrious parkee.

They strolled together until the clock tolled the hour, going through all the what-do-you-do's and where-do-you-live's and what-do-you-want-out-of-the-rest-of-your-life's—all in good time.

She protested she was too young to marry. He promised he'd get a better job. She declared she wanted to see the world. He proposed a date at the airport.

—I got a convertible. I *do!* A 1948 Cadillac—midnight green. A classic, a gem. We head out on the Belt Parkway. The stars'll be out, maybe even the moon. At Kennedy the jets are zooming in and out of the clouds all night. There's an observation deck. It's so—it's so—it's so—stupendous! When they blast off you can't hear yourself when you scream and the wind nearly blows you away. But it won't blow you away, Regina, because I'll be holding you tight!

Given the great rush, the highness of the emotional tide and Vinnie's determination not to be late again, it's hardly surprising that they failed to exchange numbers.

But Regina, promenading out of the park, scattering flowers like the Queen of the May, wasn't worried. She knew she would knock down every door in Bay Ridge to find her piece of sunshine in a powder-blue suit, Vincent J. Sciaputo.

(She promised that to the pigeons.)

When A Lady Stands Up

of
power
and
presence

Upon
occasion
a lady finds herself
in a common place, with
commonness all around. Drawing
from the deep well of dignity,
a lady's queenly presence stirs
some men's hearts
to courtly
love.

WHEN A LADY STANDS UP

Sweetly, and without regard to persons, the little lady lifted her eyes, cups of liquid ebony, and fixed them with splendid intensity on the tattooed man, and replied that she would be more than happy to oblige him when and if he ever learned what it meant to be a man and in what manner to approach a lady and until that time it behooved him to return to that damp shady spot beneath the rock from which he had crawled.

HOORAY

Thrilled to the core by such pungent eloquence, so well projected and on such a public stage, an observer at a nearby booth set his oozing jelly donut back on its plate, licked his fingers and awaited the next turn in the freshly-erupted drama.

Tattoos aside, the man was spectacle enough to stop traffic on a freeway. Massive, with shoulder-length tresses the color of summer squash, a magnificent messianic growth of beard, garbed in a lamb-white tunic that hung loosely upon him and rippled melodramatically with every gesture and every swell of his monumental chest, the man commanded attention—the way Michelangelo's David might if it were wheeled suddenly into a men's room.

To put cream on his image the man sported an "ankh," the Egyptian hieroglyph of life; which hung on a long, thick silver chain. It may have been his way of proclaiming intimacy with the occult sources of existence. Yea, he was a man of mystic significance.

What words he had spoken to the lady the prosaic patrons of that cramped, unscrubbed little coffee shop could only guess at. Whatever they were they had produced a response from her that blotched his visible skin purple as a turnip, and caused a name to drop from his lips that stopped the Muzak and set the other *caballeros* there (including the Ethiopian chef who was usually imperturbable as a boulder in raging whitewater) to flexing their biceps and rubbing their knuckles meditatively.

But, as it turned out, there was no need for knights and swords, for the lady stood up.

Yes, she stood up, her eyes about level with the man's mystic ankh. She sighed, and looked up at the ersatz prophet, that erstwhile propheteer. She looked steadily and deeply into his opaque blue eyes.

In the midst of our rattling world, a long silence was extruded. The long silence was broken by a cough and a convulsive blinking from the man. Abashed, he gave a scornful snort or two. He lifted his hand threateningly. She looked at it. He brushed back his long locks, as if all his intentions were innocent and had always been so.

Never once did she turn, never once did she look about for assistance, though she would have had a score at her side had she signalled, a score of men who recognized quality when they saw it.

She was chic—in green—skirt and jacket—heels—beyond fashion—a woman of purpose. On her way to *somewhere*. Attractive, though not pretty; trim and well-formed, though not voluptuous—classical. She had *something* all right.

Perhaps it was dignity.

Ultimately, the tunicked, tattooed hulk shrugged and gave a slovenly wave that was meant to express his disappointment with the absurd and faithless ways of this world. As he passed a nearby booth the man with the doughnut noticed that despite his jaunty, irrepressible air there was perplexity swimming in his shallow eyes.

She left shortly thereafter, looking as if nothing at all had occurred. She smiled at the sweating busboy who rushed to hold the door for her. He was a busboy much-envied.

They all tried to catch her eye but she was looking elsewhere. They watched her walk to her white Corvette and as she wheeled out of the lot onto the main road, her road, they noted the appropriateness of the three letters of her license plate.

They spelled out E V E.

My Wife, My Life

a second look

Oh,
how hurry
and familiarity
dull things, even a thing
as bright and dear as love. Herein,
a married man attests to the
tarnish that has come
over his life—his
wife.

MY WIFE, MY LIFE

Sometimes you forget. You know how it is: time and the press of events push, pin and scuttle you and you forget what's under your nose. You don't notice it; you take it for granted. Happens all the time. Even with something you always wanted, something you ached for, something, maybe, that you went all out to get.

> Like a wife.

If ever I had something sacred, something past price, something stupendous, it was her. It *is* her. Yet, most times I give as much notice to her as I give to the scatter-rug in the hall.

She does what she has to do, I do what I have to do and when I come home I kiss her dutifully, eat the meal she's cooked, listen to her account of her day, with its peaks and tribulations, tell her a thing or two about what happened to me, watch some TV and call it a day. We call it a day, we call it a year, we call it a lifetime.

But if you ask me what does she look like or if I've seen her eyes lately or how has she been feeling... really, I don't know if I can answer. I mean, I know I *can't* answer. She's just there, my wife. My eyes are usually on the meatballs and if my shirt's been pressed.

To see this dreamy travesty you'd never believe that once upon a rainbow she was my all-in-all, she was the one that I was going to tear down the stars for. You'd never believe that she was the one that I went to such lengths to persuade to marry me.

That's how it goes. What I wanted, I have. But I don't *have it*, because I don't notice it. She's some sort of vagary, my wife. She's in and around my life and only occasionally impinges on me, like a crick in the neck.

I suppose most everything is that way. The precious and the cherished turn familiar and, sadly, cease to be what they were. Particularly when it comes to wives and kids— or husbands and kids—or dogs and cats—or anything, any of those precious, priceless things.

To lose what you have because you lose sight of it or lose touch with it or forget about it or neglect it may well be the worst, most tragic way of missing the boat.

But last night my wife—who's a great

one for responding to her inspirations—took out the wedding pictures, our own wedding pictures, slides, and threw them up on the wall. I hadn't seen those pictures in years and years.

It's hard to believe I was ever that young. We all looked so young then. My kid brother looked like a kid. My nephews had round faces. My mother looked pretty, not so worried, not so drained of hope. Friends, all of them, looked like little boys and girls.

At the core of the affair was a gorgeous girl in a white dress and white veil and blue-as-the-sky eyes. Dancing in this picture, laughing in that, serious at the altar, glorious when her big brothers lifted her up on their shoulders.

Her beauty was the axis of the whole event. It gave life and light and meaning to it, her beauty that had once so captured my heart I wanted it near me day and night, her beauty that has never dimmed.

Of all those pictures the one that struck me deepest was the one of her looking out of the back window of the limo that whisked us from the church to the reception hall. Smiling and waving, her radiance framed by lacy white modesty. She was everything, everything I had ever wanted.

I turned and stole a look at her as she was clicking the carousel of slides last night. Ah, she is beyond compare.

She is more lovely than the lilacs in spring, she is peaches and plums and passion fruit, she is the same shining splendor I rode off with in the car, into the night, into the new life I had always hoped for.

Sometimes you remember.

Autumn Love

in due season

Love
being without
a timetable cannot be
confined to a single season,
not even spring. When it comes
in the glow of autumn love's
embrace is long and
quiet and
deep.

AUTUMN LOVE

They were walking in the garden,
her garden.
She was showing him
the pumpkins among the cornstalks,
marvelous immensities of orange,
the grandest she'd ever grown
in all the years she'd kept the garden.

They talked softly, among
long silences;

their minds on other things;
other things still unspoken.

There was a muskiness in the noon air,
   the sun, vigorous and glittering,
   hung idly in a crystal sky,
   a haze drifted aimlessly
   through the heavy ripeness
   of her autumn garden.

The world was mellow,
   it was warm.
   Still, in the soft core
   of the golden Indian summer,
   one sensed the knives of winter
   being honed.
   Nothing bound to the circling seasons
   lasts for long.

He stood laced in a lingering silence,
   his head drooping,
   like her sunflowers.
   She finished some wayward
   sentence she had started,

then she, too, lapsed
into an uncertain quiet.

A hum—the buzz and grumble
of many wings—ruled over that
wavering moment,
a dying moment in the dying season.

The two felt awkward suddenly.
He stared at the ground,
his eye following the desperate movements
of a limping cricket.
He rubbed the stubble of his beard,
roughly, pointlessly, till his cheek
turned red and blotched.
She sighed and moved her head
languorously,
stealing a long look at him—
a tall man, sturdy,
a face bony and creviced
like an outcropping of rock;
a gentleman.

"I don't know what it is," she said abruptly,

HOORAY

"what it is that makes us different;
not just you and me but
a man and a woman.
I don't mean outwardly,
I mean the deep down inside us
that makes us—
one a man, one a woman,
my nature, your nature..."

He didn't answer her.   Instead
he began to drift away from her
and the long shadow
she made on the brown soil,
and as he moved away from her
he gathered courage to move further,
then further.

He had wanted a woman to cook,
to keep house, to make a home,
not a woman that thought
and mulled and asked
odd, ungainly questions.
When she spoke like she had
just done he became uneasy,

and though he could not admit it
to himself
it made him afraid.

After he had passed through the gate
he looked back, at her
and her garden.
She was standing still
as the corn stalks stand.
He strode to his truck, stumbling
in his haste on a rock
he had stumbled on before.

Marriage was a foolish thing,
he thought; unnatural,
a priest-inspired thing.
He was content living alone
with his father,
sullen and crusty as he was,
content with working the apple orchards,
pruning, spraying, picking;
content with a good pipeful
by the black wood-stove

on the windy winter nights.

Before he reached his truck
  he heard behind him the rush
  of her footsteps;
  before he opened the door
  he saw her in the mirror,
  racing toward the gate.
  His breath was lopped short,
  his heart beat too hard
  sending shudders to his extremities.
  He was helpless as a child again,
  helpless before the force
  of his body's responses.

She never looked at him
  but went running over the road
  and down into the embrace
  of a wide, unharvested rye field,
  her long lavender dress rippling,
  her brown hair loose and long.

She was so unlike all those women
  he had met in shopping centers,

AUTUMN LOVE

    in slacks, smoking cigarettes, bold.
    She was so different,
    so real.
    His legs, moving with their own will,
    took him after her.

She fell in the rye field, stumbling
   over a stone.
   She'd hurt her knee.
   He came near her, looked to her,
   yet all he did was shake his head.
   "I waited so long for you," she cried.
   "I'm tired of it. Of it all.
   Go home to your father
   and drink your ginger beer
   and smoke your pipe.
   Go away from my life."

He did. Slowly, like a horse
  dragging a hearse,
  he went to his car.
  He sat in it a long time,
  his forehead pressed

HOORAY

   against the cold steering wheel.

The indifferent dark, blank
   and uneventful behind his closed eyes,
   gave him some comfort.
   After a while, he knew not how long,
   he heard her footsteps on the gravel.
   He heard the door shut, and thought
   he could hear her
   climbing the stairs.
   He wondered if she had locked
   the door to her house.
   He rubbed his hands as he walked
   doggedly to the door
   to try the latch.
   The blood had emptied out of his hands.
   The doorknob metal was warm.
   He contemplated his vague reflection
   in the glass of her front door.
   Never, he thought to himself,
   never had such a stupid man
   ever been born.

He turned the knob,

the door opened.
His heart became bathed
in the warm waters of gratitude
for such a thing as an unlocked door.

She had two cups set out
  on the kitchen table,
  the coffee was steaming in the cups.
  There was a napkin and milk and sugar
  at his usual place.
  How could she have done so much
  in so short a time?
  He was full of wonder.
  She knew that he would come.
  She was magical.
  She always knew.

She never looked his way.
  She was extraordinarily busy.
  He fell into his chair.
  The smell of the coffee seemed to him
  the smell of paradise.
  She said, "Do you want some
  pie or anything?"

HOORAY

"Just sit down," he said gruffly.

They looked at one another
across her long trestle table.
Before the words came out
of the man's mouth
some sounds issued,
odd agonized sounds.
At last:
"I want you to marry me."
"No, no." She insisted, shaking her head.
"Not if you can't ask
any better than that."

He'd been pouring milk from the pitcher
when he spoke,
perhaps that's what bothered her.
But he understood for once.
And he nodded.

She was staring at the wood-grain
of the table and waiting.
He looked at her,
at her handsome face,

freckled and barely lined,
at her modest, generous presence.
She drew him to her
like a magnet draws iron,
like the stall draws the horse home,
like water draws the thirsty deer
down from the hills.

"When I see you I see myself.
You understand?"

The words cracked the wall of his heart.
He could say no more.

Her eyes closed and tears rolled
out of them and down
her cheeks and fell
in droplets
on her lap.

He watched her in an admiration
close to worship.
He waited.

He forgot about the coffee,
   he forgot about his house
   and his father
   and all the apples
   in his orchard,
   he forgot about everything
   including time.

He sat quietly,
   head bowed
   hands clasped
   upon the tabletop.

He waited
   for some answer
   to come
   from her
   to him.

Her answer came
   in the form of a smile,
   a slow smile
   unfolding
   upon her gleaming
   golden face.

Without opening her eyes,
   she reached
   across the table to him,
   tentatively
   like someone reaching
   in a pitch-black tunnel,
   until
   she found his hand.

O Fathomless Love

a search against the tide

The ocean said to me once,
"Look!
Yonder on the shore
Is a woman, weeping.
I have watched her.
Go you and tell her this—
Her lover I have laid
In cool green hall.
There is wealth of golden sand
And pillars, coral-red;
Two white fish stand guard at his bier.

"Tell her this
And more—
That the king of the seas
Weeps too, old, helpless man.
The bustling fates
Heap his hands with corpses
Until he stands like a child
With surplus of toys."

—from Stephen Crane's *The Black Riders*

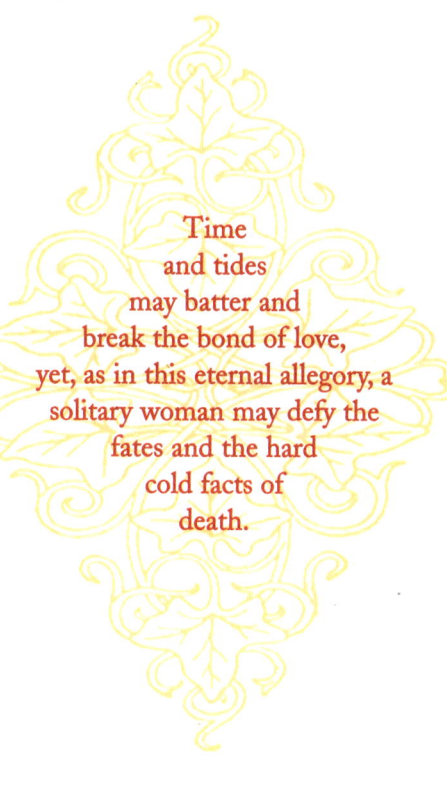

Time
and tides
may batter and
break the bond of love,
yet, as in this eternal allegory, a
solitary woman may defy the
fates and the hard
cold facts of
death.

THE STORY

A young woman, whose husband has been lost at sea, sets out to find his body. She scours the ocean floor. There she encounters the King of the Seas. He asserts his lawful and immutable claim upon the body. But she persists.

People imagine plays are hard to read, but everyone has all the imagination they need.

O FATHOMLESS LOVE

PERSONS

The King of the Seas (*an ancient*)
Teresa (*a young widow*)
Emmanuel (*a young sailor*)

SCENE.—*The Bottom of the Sea.*

The waves shimmer in a dim aquamarine light. Here are fantastical coral shapes, the passing shadows of restless fish, and a dense, terrific silence. Here and there, a frail sunbeam falls.

Dozing on a throne-like rock is the hoary old King of the Seas. His seaweed entangled hair is topped by a crown. He holds a rusty trident.

Through the waters, a woman's voice calls forlornly.

TERESA
Emmanuel...Emmanuel...

Her cries awaken the King. Annoyed, he looks around and spies the approaching woman. He leaves his throne, and crouches behind it, hiding his crown and trident.

A young, beautiful woman appears. She wears a white blouse and skirt trimmed with roses, a peasant's dress. Her dark eyes are hollow with longing.

TERESA

In a sobbing whisper.

Oh Emmanuel, my Emmanuel, where have you gone from me?

Leaning wearily against some coral.

These seas are so long, love; this ocean floor is so wide.

THE KING

In hiding.

These waters are quite wet enough, madam, and there's enough salt here to burn a person's eyes without you adding your tears to it.

TERESA

Startled.

Who said that? Where are you?

She looks around.

Won't you come out?

KING

If you promise to stop that infernal wailing and weeping.

TERESA

I'll try, though I don't know what else I can do.

KING

Sticking his head up.
You can always jump over the moon.

TERESA

Why, you silly old man, what are you doing back there?

KING

Oh, I amuse you, do I?
Strutting importantly.
I would have you know you're not just talking to any old body!

TERESA

Abashed.
I'm sorry, sir, you surprised me. Who are you?

KING
I? Who am I? I—uh—uh—I am . . . *nobody*!

TERESA
Nobody isn't a *real* name.

KING
Ah, but it tells a real story. But you, who are you, who come slobbering and slaughtering the silence?

TERESA
Teresa's my name. Though it hardly matters. You, whoever *you* are, do you live down here?

KING
Peevishly.
I do, I do. If you can call this miserable soggy existence living. What do you want down here?

TERESA
Sobbing.
I'm looking for my husband, Emman—

KING

Don't start that blubbering again.

TERESA

Bravely.

My husband, my Emmanuel. Have you seen him?

KING

Nothing but fins and fishes here.

TERESA

He was lost in a storm yesterday. His boat came to shore empty. He has to be down here somewhere.

KING

If he's dead what matter? Dead in water, dead on land. The dead are dead and no longer stand.

TERESA

Until I find his body, till I see and touch him, I will not believe he is dead.

KING

Forget him, Teresa. Make the best of what you have. Wait for his body to wash up on the shore. And stay away from fishermen. They're all fools—thinking they can gamble and win on the water.

TERESA

He knew the ways of the wind and the ways of the waves better than any man in our village. My Emmanuel is a very, very great sailor.

KING

Mocking.

Aye, they are all "very great sailors." You poor women are as dream-soaked as your men.

TERESA

Holding back her sobs.

Won't you help me, sir? I've turned this cruel ocean inside out like an old shirt, but I can't—I can't—

She breaks into tears.

KING

Distraught.
Oh stop. Please. I can't take all this emotion.
Taking Teresa by the hand.
Come, come sit here on my—on this rock.

TERESA

For just a moment then.

KING

What else have we but moments—long or short or eternal?

TERESA

You're a strange old man, sometimes you seem cruel, sometimes you seem kind.

KING

I'm kind—always kind—too kind.

TERESA

Impatiently.
I must go. I must find him.

KING
He won't run away from his watery grave.

TERESA
Getting up.
Then you know where he is . . . ?

KING
Evasively.
I mean it metaphorically. Now I ask you to sit, so sit! You have no manners, my dear girl. So noisy, so persistent—

TERESA
Pathetically.
Why are you so cross with me?

KING
Cross?! I'm kind to you. I am trying to preserve you from pain, unnecessary pain.

TERESA
I don't want to be preserved. You're as cruel as the sea. You know where he is and you won't tell me!

KING

Threateningly.

You are trying my patience, young woman. Beware—if you hope to get home again.

TERESA

Frightened.

I didn't mean to offend you.

KING

Scornfully.

Bah, you can't offend me, little fool. I am beyond flattery and blame.

Gently.

You know you have no right to be down here, picking among the shreds of the dead.

TERESA

Without him I am an empty basket.

KING

Other women lose lovers; they still live. So has it been since this miserable world was made, and so will it be until it gets unmade.

TERESA

How little you know of women. They breathe; they don't live! They die day by day. If you know where he is, tell me.

KING

Sharply.
I know that women belong in their kitchens.
He sighs.
Teresa, Teresa, why did he have to raise sail—with a red sky and whitecaps and the wind howling and battering the shore?

TERESA

Emmanuel says a good sailor is not afraid of the weather.

KING

Then our dear Emmanuel deserved what he got. Justice is just.

TERESA

Pleading.
No, no!

KING

It is the law—and it is iron.

TERESA

Doesn't love matter? Doesn't the law ever take love into account? He was fishing for us, for his family, for me—out of love.

KING

On the scale love weighs less than a sparrow's feather. You ask too much, Teresa. The world and its laws can't step aside for love. Because he loves, because you love. Bah, he should have stood home, out of the reach of the fates.

TERESA

You do know! Don't lie! Tell me where he is! Why do you want to keep me from him?

KING

Reluctantly.

I know the waves formed a curled coffin for him. I know he settled to the sea's floor like a falling leaf.

TERESA
Appealing.
Where is that place, old one? Tell me.

KING
Coldly.
He belongs to the sea now!

TERESA
Defiantly.
He belongs to me! To me!

KING
No, he belongs to me!!

TERESA
To you?!! Why to you?

KING
I meant the sea. That's what I meant. He belongs—

TERESA
No, you meant what you said. Why do you keep lying to me? Why were you hiding? Who are

you? What are you doing down here? Why are you trying to stop me? You nasty, mean old man!

KING

Back-pedalling.
You impertinent little snipe! You go too far with me!

TERESA

You can't frighten me anymore.
Teresa starts to leave.

KING

Wait; where are you going?

TERESA

Bitterly.
Thank you for breaking your precious silence with all your comforting conversation.

KING

Shouting after her.
You'll be making circles into nowhere. There's nothing down here but sand and stone and the dark cold arms of the sea.

TERESA

I'd rather *try* and fail than bow down to fate—or your rusty iron laws.

KING

Chiding.
Sure, you think you can wish anything into being—like a new dress at Easter time.
Teresa turns and leaves.
You are a willful, stupid girl!

TERESA

Moaning.
Emmanuel…Emmanuel…

KING

Calling after her.
Not that way, you fool! You won't even find the shadow of your beloved out there.

Teresa returns.

TERESA

Coyly.
Which way shall I go then?

KING

Damn you, you play on my heart strings! You're not as innocent as you seem. And don't smirk at me either.

TERESA

But you're such a funny old man.

KING

Softening.
You won't get your way with me. You women, you think you can have anything you want just because you are full of love! Baah, love is a dream.

TERESA

Impatiently.
Well…?

KING

Well what?

TERESA

Playfully.
"Baah," which way should I walk?

KING

Questions, questions, that's all you humans have are questions!

TERESA

Yes, and you never answer any of them!

> *Flustered, the King moves around his throne and absent-mindedly picks up his trident.*

KING

What you don't seem to understand—which I am trying repeatedly to make clear to you—is that there are laws—irreversible procedures!

TERESA

I don't care about such things.

KING

Exasperated.

Of course not. If it were up to you the tides, the stars, the sharks would arrange themselves to please you and your darling love.

TERESA

Why do you bother to talk to me then? You're no help.

Pointing to his trident.
What is that you're holding?

KING

This? Just a piece of old iron. I'll tell you why I talk to you—because I'm foolish and gone to taffy in the brain—like the dolphins in the month of May. There, I've answered a question!

TERESA

Is *that* true?

KING

Another question?! Is *what* true?

TERESA

Really, why do you keep talking to me? Why do you keep pretending to help me? What are you doing here in the first place? You were waiting for me, weren't you? What do you want from me?

KING

Lying again.
If you must know I was sent to you.

TERESA
Sent to me? Who sent you?

KING
That decrepit old greybeard, the King of these stupid seas—who sends me on all his sentimental, infernal errands.

TERESA
Warily.
The King of the Seas cares about me?

KING
Well, the weepy old fool saw you wailing on the shore and he saw you wade into his Kingdom, and he hasn't been able to sleep a decent wink with all your yowling and moaning.

TERESA
Why did he send *you* . . . ?

KING

He's too lazy to come himself.
> *Laughing.*

Oh, you should see how old and waterlogged the duffer has become; how his rickety old bones creak in the sea-swell.

TERESA

Poor old man. I want to go to him.

KING

> *Firmly.*

You can't go to him. And don't waste your pity. He's as foremost a fool as you and your great sailor of a husband.

TERESA

Why do you insult him so?

KING

> *Scornfully.*

If you think I'm impossible you should meet *him*. Yes, you should have an audience with *him*.

TERESA
I don't think you're impossible...

KING
Rambling on.
You'd think after all these centuries of gulping, drowning men he'd learn something. He still weeps with the widows. He imagines he understands human grief and can soothe souls as he does his precious fish. Pisssh.

TERESA
Slyly.
And is this *his* throne?

KING
Lying through his teeth.
This? No, this is just a rock.

TERESA
Pisssh. It looks like a throne.

KING
It does?

TERESA
Yes. Very like a throne.

KING
Pretending to examine the throne.

Well, it could be a throne, I suppose. But as I was saying, he saw you and said to me: "Look. Yonder on the shore is a woman weeping. I have watched her. Go you and tell her this—" That's how he talks to me, as if he were addressing a whole court—

TERESA
And tell me what?

KING
Irritated.

Ye Gods, are you impatient! I'll tell you, if I'm given half a chance. Let's pretend we're in his throne room.

In mocking tones.

"Go you and tell her this: Her lover I have laid in cool green hall. There is wealth of golden sand and pillars, coral-red; two white fish stand guard at his bier." That's what he said. He talks like he's reciting poetry.

TERESA
Thoughtfully.
It's very beautiful. . .what he said.

KING
But not very comforting. That's it. Then he rolled back to sleep—his favorite occupation.

TERESA
Sympathetically.
Why does he sleep so much?

KING
The poor devil's lonely. Wouldn't you be lonely out here in this soulless, godforsaken wasteland, with only the swish of fins going by and the far-off crashing of waves—waves eternally crashing under a cold-hearted moon.

TERESA
Can he be as lonely as I am who have lost my self—my life—my Emmanuel!

KING

He's a god, you have to understand that, and he has no one but himself. He's more lonely than a sunken galleon loaded with pearls that not even the squid care to look at anymore.

TERESA

No, my loneliness is worse. He has schools of bluefish and whales and dolphins and chests full of the souls of ships and sailors . . . I am a silly starfish that the waves have flung high upon the beach. If he knew that, he would help me.

KING

Fatherly.
He knows what's best. Go home, Teresa.

TERESA

*Sinking to her knees like a suppliant
before a king.*
What will I do? How will I live? I need him, I need him!

KING

Wait, my dear, till the end of the world when the angels lift up Atlantis and unhinge the graves on land and sea. Then you'll have your precious Emmanuel.

TERESA

Grasping the King's legs.

I cannot wait so long, your Highness. Help me. *You* are the King of the Seas. You can help me. Please, I want to see him.

KING

Smiling.

Ah, Teresa, Teresa. A fool can't fool anyone. Please don't cry anymore. No more tears. Learn patience and wait. Eternity will come soon enough.

Tears are in his eyes, too.

Look at me. Crying doesn't help.

He wipes her tears.

Yes, my dear, the King of the Seas weeps, too. Behold, my kingdom—all this wondrous waste, this boundless bitterness. And I am bound to it till the world's end.

The King puts on his crown.

TERESA

Why did you hide yourself from me? I wouldn't have been so disrespectful to you.
Chastising him.
But you know it is a sinful thing to pretend to be something other than you are.

KING

It is, it is. But isn't it what we all do? Isn't it the game we all play? You're looking better now. Do you feel better?

TERESA

Nodding.
Better, yes. But not well.

KING

Dramatically.
"They heap my hands with corpses,
 the bustling fates, until I stand
 like a child with surplus of toys."
There, that sounds a little like poetry, doesn't it?

TERESA
Why do you stay down here, Your Highness? This is a terrible job.

KING
Smiling sadly.
It is, but it is my job. I absorb the suffering of sailors and wives and all those lost at sea. Their suffering must go somewhere. I watch—as they drown and a bubble comes to their mouths, as the wet-eyed women scour the cold horizon, as the lost children whimper in the night. I sleep most of the time, and that helps me to bear it.

TERESA
My father, too, was drowned. Francesco was his name.

KING
He was a handsome man, and tall.

TERESA
You remember him?

KING
Who can forget all those many men—fishing for love?

TERESA
My mother must have felt as I do. I understand her better now.

KING
She did not come to search my seas, though.

TERESA
She talked always of my father and told us over and over again all the stories he used to tell. He once hooked a whale, he said, but it got away. But it was true—don't laugh. Each night—without fail—we'd hear her sobbing through the walls, my little sister and I.
She sighs.
She could never forget him. Never.

KING
Very few things last as long as never.

TERESA

Lost in her memories.

My Emmanuel brought me on his boat the very first day we were married. I was not ashamed to look at him, bare-chested, brown and sweating—struggling with the sunny, windy sea. Hauling up his nets. Coming home under full sail. How fine he looked. I always remember him that way as I wait and stir his supper. He was more handsome than my father. The look in his eye on the sea that day was the same strong sure look he had when he held me close. How can I forget him?

KING

Tenderly.

Teresa, you make too many tears inside you. You will make yourself a sad old age.

TERESA

It would not be sad to grow old if I could grow old with him. If I could have. And I would not care a fig about dying if we could share the same grave. Do you understand how I feel?

KING
Sagely.
Yes, yes, but youth has a short memory.

TERESA
I will not forget him!

KING
I, too, was young once, Teresa, swimming in great hopes. I don't even remember now what they were. I settled for the surge of the sea. I had to do something. I did this. And I've gotten gray in the beard.

TERESA
Turning away.
I will not listen to you.

KING
Then listen to that. Listen, listen. That's the swing of the sea. Like music it has a lilt. Hear it? I listen to it when I'm sad. It's very comforting.
Touching her.
Teresa, don't be mad at me, an old man. . .

TERESA

Softening.

There are shells on our beach that the children hold to their ears, saying they are listening to the ocean tell secrets. But our little Pietro and Maria don't care about such things anymore.

Peering into the King's eyes.

Can't you let me at least look at him before I go?

KING

I've done more than I should have already.

TERESA

I just want to see his face—one more time. One more time, one look at my Emmanuel's face…

KING

One look is all?

TERESA

Yes, *one look* and I'll leave.

KING

I had hoped to spare you this.

TERESA
Horrified.
Has he been chewed by the sharks?!

KING
No, no. He is as he was. I mean that you'll look but you'll want another look. And next you'll want to take him back. But I cannot give him to you, no matter how much you beg me, or how fond I am of you. The dead and the drowned belong to me and to the sea. I cannot give them back. Remember this, Teresa.

TERESA
Undaunted.
Come then, show him to me. I am ready.

KING
Rising from his throne.
He's cold now, and still, very still. No longer warm anymore as he was, as you knew him. You must prepare yourself, Teresa. You'll find him to be pale, too. And . . . different. Though content to be out of the wind's way.

TERESA
Do you think he has forgotten me?

KING
As soon as his lungs filled and the blackness overcame him. Come take my hand.
> *Tentatively, Teresa takes his hand, and he leads her slowly through blue waters.*

TERESA
What is the good of living if we die and forget those we love?

KING
That's a good question to ask the gods.

TERESA
I don't believe he has forgotten me.

KING
You can believe what you wish.

TERESA
I want to know the truth, not just believe.

KING

I can tell you he is not the man you knew. He is stone. And at rest. Part of the great sea now.

> *Teresa's chest heaves with great sobs.*

Why are you crying? This is the truth.

TERESA

> *Pleading.*

Please, don't keep me from him any longer.

KING

Close your eyes, Teresa.

> *A shaft of honey-colored light reveals Emmanuel's bier. There are, as the King said, the coral-red pillars, the two white fish, the golden sand. Bare-chested, in blue sailor's pants, arms at his sides, lies the man. His eyes are closed. He is as pale and still as marble.*

Open your eyes. He's here.

> *Teresa takes a moment to gather her courage.*

TERESA
That's not him! That's not Emmanuel!

KING
I warned you he would be different.

TERESA
Dear God, he's so white, so pale.
Approaching him.
He looks like he's only asleep.

KING
Yes. In a certain sense he is.

TERESA
May I touch him?

KING
Exasperated.
See?! You said a *look*. Just a look!

TERESA
Quietly persistent.
One touch wouldn't matter.

KING
Sighing.
If you wish to suffer even more...
> *Teresa approaches the bier and touches the limp fingers of Emmanuel.*

TERESA
Aghast.
He's cold. He's so cold.

KING
As I warned you...

TERESA
Accusingly.
What have you done to him?

KING
I? I?!

TERESA
Oh, you've murdered him! Oh, my Emmanuel! You've murdered him, you and your iron laws! Oh my darling, my dearest!

KING
I have done nothing, Teresa.

TERESA
Wildly.
You have, you have! You've taken the fire from him!

KING
I take what the fates give me.

TERESA
Raging.
Who are the fates?! What rights do they have over a man?! I don't believe in your "fates"!

KING
Teresa, you're making more misery for yourself.

TERESA
On wings of power.
I love him, you King of the Seas! I love him! I will not let you have him! Don't you understand, I cannot be separated from him!

KING
Taking her hand.
Come now, my dear.

TERESA
Breaking away from him.
No, I am not your "dear"!
She seizes Emmanuel.
Emmanuel, can you hear me? It's your Teresa. Don't let them do this to you! Emmanuel, I've come so far for you! Do you hear me, love?
She shakes him wildly.
Emmanuel! Emmanuel!
The King of the Seas wags his head with great weariness.

TERESA
Oh, dearest, open your eyes for me! Wake up, wake up for me! Wake up for your Teresa!

KING
Sitting down on a rock.
The stones and the Spanish gold that sleeps under the sea will wake sooner than he.

TERESA
Fiercely.
Don't try to stop me!

KING
Indifferently.
No need. I can wait till you're done.

TERESA
You hear him, love? He's mocking us. Show him your strength; show him how much you love me. Respond to me! I'm calling to you! Open your eyes and look at me.

KING
You see. You see. You're talking to a stone.

TERESA
Taunting him.
You won't open your eyes because you don't love me. Your whispers were lies and your fine words were empty as the wind. Had you really loved me you would have clung to the mast and you would have come home to me—

Imploring him.
My dearest, my dearest don't leave me to a black dress and an empty, cold bed.
She makes the sign of the cross.

KING

Have you received your answer, Teresa?

TERESA

He's there. He's *in* there, in that chest.

KING

He's a dead man, Teresa. A cold corpse. Come, come away, in time you will forget him.

TERESA

If I ever forget this man they should drag me through the streets of the town, and throw me down from the cliffs and leave me there till the gulls peck the heart out of me!

She touches his forehead.

His forehead is warm. It feels warm. I think he is warm!

KING
Dubiously.
Yes, yes.

TERESA
It is, I'm telling you!

KING
Your imagination is what is warm, Teresa. Come, enough of this.

TERESA
No, feel it. Please, feel it. He's in here. He's in here, he's in this body! I can feel him! Emmanuel, he doesn't believe me! Are you coming out or aren't you? If you want to stay sleeping, I'll go home without you.
Ecstatically.
There, there! His eyelid twitched!

KING
Dissuadingly.
Teresa, Teresa.

TERESA
His hand just moved! Did you see it?!

KING

A trick of light on the water.

TERESA

Rubbing Emmanuel's hands.

Feel his hand. It's warm. He *is* trying to come back. He wants to come home with me.

Confronting the King.

If he's alive he doesn't have to stay here—isn't that true?!

KING

Yes, only the dead belong to me—and the mad, the lunatic.

TERESA

Testing.

If he wakes up, will you stop us, King of the Seas?

The King doesn't answer.

Will you?

KING

After a long silence.

If he can walk then he's yours . . .

TERESA
Massaging him.
You're getting warmer and warmer. Work harder, dear. Your life is coming back like the spring.
> *She embraces him and kisses him,*
> *smothering him with kisses.*

Mmm, how warm your lips are love. Hold me, hold me, hold me.
> *She wraps his limp arms around her.*

O my Emmanuel! You are the blood of my blood. You are the life of my life.
> *For a moment everything under the sea*
> *becomes preternaturally still. Then,*
> *Emmanuel's arm lifts by itself,*
> *and grasps Teresa.*

KING
O my blessed soul, he moved his arm!

TERESA
Jubilant.
He did! You saw it, didn't you?! Oh my darling, open your eyes!
> *As if she is waking him in the morning.*

Time to open your eyes—Emmanuel.
Beckoning to the King.
He's trying. Come closer, Your Highness, come and see.
Emmanuel groans sleepily.
Did you hear that, Your Highness?

KING

Feigning grumpiness.
I heard it. How could I help hearing it?

TERESA

That's the way he moans in the morning.
Hugging him.
Oh, my dear, how I love the noises you make.
Taking the King's hand.
Come feel how warm his flesh is under your cold ocean.

KING

Reluctantly touching Emmanuel.
Yes, yes.

TERESA

Isn't he warm? And when his eyes open you'll see how blue they are.

KING

He is very warm.

TERESA

You see?!

KING

Playfully.
I do. And now do you see why I don't like this just-one-look business?

TERESA

Laughing and hugging the King.
Oh, my sweet, sweet King!

KING

Enigmatically.
I see. *You* see. But will *he* ever see?

TERESA

Sobered for a moment.
What do you mean?

KING

Will he ever see how powerful love is? *Your* love? Your love that is bringing him back to life, that probably made a man of him in the first place. Do you think *he* will see—ever?

TERESA

Breezily.
Of course, of course he'll see, you silly old King.

KING

Of course, of course.

EMMANUEL

Groaning and stretching.
Teresa, what time is it?

TERESA

Time to rise, Blue-eyes.

EMMANUEL

Oooh, my bones grind and groan like an old ship. I must be getting old, my sweet.

TERESA

You have slept too long, my sleepyhead, and too, too deep.

EMMANUEL
Opening his eyes.
I never get enough sleep. Where the devil are we?

TERESA
Cheerily.
Under the sea. That's where we are.

EMMANUEL
Under the sea. Oh, well, that's nice.
He closes his eyes and rolls over to sleep some more.

TERESA
Oh, no, no. You can't go back to sleep.

EMMANUEL
Sleepily.
Five more. Five more minutes. Wake me in…

His words trail off in a sleepy mumble.

TERESA
No, darling, you can't go back!
Shaking him.

KING
Damn fool! He's dropping off. If he goes now, he'll never come back.

TERESA
Wake up, Emmanuel! Please, wake up!

KING
What kind of a man do you have here?
Slapping Emmanuel.
Wake up, you idiot.

EMMANUEL
Ooh, that hurt, Teresa. You hit too hard.

TERESA
Pulling him into a sitting position.
You're getting up right now.

EMMANUEL
But it's so sweet to sleep on Sundays.

TERESA
Unrelentingly.
But it's not Sunday, dumbhead. It's Wednesday.

EMMANUEL
Bolting up.
Wednesday?! How can it be Wednesday?!
Emmanuel rouses himself.

TERESA
You have to dress and get your nets ready and pull your boat into the water. The sun's out. Another beautiful day to fish. When you come back tonight you'll be smiling and your nets will be full.

EMMANUEL
Another long, hard day.
Taking her hand.
You, Teresa, make everything sound so nice.

TERESA

Buoyantly.

I will wait on the shore for you. I'll wave as you come in. Pietro and Maria will run down to meet you.

EMMANUEL

Yes, where are those two little sweetpeas?

TERESA

They're out playing already. I'll have a potful of chicken soup ready for you.
Mischievously.
You still like chicken soup, don't you?

EMMANUEL

Fading again.
I do, yes. Ooooh.
Teresa stops him from falling back.

TERESA

Help me, Your Highness!

KING
Furiously.
Stand up, Emmanuel, before I poke you with my fork. Stand up and be a man!

EMMANUEL
Opening his eyes wide.
Who is this?!

KING
You just get up and get out of here! I've wasted enough time on the two of you. You've got work to do today! And so do I.

EMMANUEL
Go check the calendar, go, go. If it's a saint's day, I don't have to work. Check the calendar, Teresa.

KING
Oh, he's too tired to work. Like an old lady—an old washerwoman.

EMMANUEL
Indignant.
I never get tired. I can fish for a week without

sleep. I'm strong. I can work through storms and hot sun. I'm a man.

KING

Then act like one. You moan too much.

EMMANUEL

This is a rude old pickle, Teresa. If I didn't respect the elderly and decrepit I'd punch him in the nose.

KING

You proud little fool, you don't know how lucky you are.

The King walks away.

TERESA

Don't talk to him like that. Don't talk to one another like that.

EMMANUEL

Let him talk.

TERESA
Where are you going?

EMMANUEL
Teresa, just lift me a little.
Standing up, but wobbly.
Too much sleep is worse than too little.
Teresa steadies him.
Mmm, not a man, huh? We will see. Today I'll bring in the biggest fish ever. I'll bring in a whale!

TERESA
Calling the King.
Don't go away now! Please come back!

EMMANUEL
Did the babies eat?

TERESA
Oh, yes.

EMMANUEL
Grabbing her.
Give me a nice wet kiss to start the day.
They kiss.

Teresa, my love, you are more tasty than a loaf of bread.

TERESA
Pushing him away playfully.
Always the same silly words.

EMMANUEL
Silly, yes. But true also.

TERESA
Come, let's walk to the shore.

EMMANUEL
I had a terrible dream, Teresa. I think that's what made me feel so heavy and made my head stuff up with cotton. I dreamt I drowned. There was a storm. I tried to sail through it, to get home, but the waves pulled me down, down into the sea. Oooh, this head of mine feels like a wet shoe. It could have been the wine last night. If I ever take another drink, you give me a kick, o.k.?

TERESA
A good swift kick.

EMMANUEL
Where did that old geezer go?

TERESA
Who knows where he goes? We have a long way to walk.

EMMANUEL
Today will be a glorious day. We will beat the sea today.

They start to walk, arm in arm.

TERESA
Your head will dry in the sun.

EMMANUEL
And I will catch you a big fish today, my love, my Teresa.

TERESA
My Emmanuel.

They kiss and kiss.

EMMANUEL
Let's go, or I will waste the whole day kissing you.

TERESA
That would not be bad.
Once more Teresa calls out to the King.
Thank you, Ocean! Thank you, dear King of the Seas!

EMMANUEL
Come and sing me one of your songs, Teresa.

TERESA
Improvising.
Oh, the morning sun is bright and golden.
The sky and sea are blue above.
Another day we have together,
Me and my dearest love . . .

> *They walk off. The light shrinks to a single beam that shines upon the King of the Seas, who sits on his throne—smiling.*

LIGHTS GO DOWN

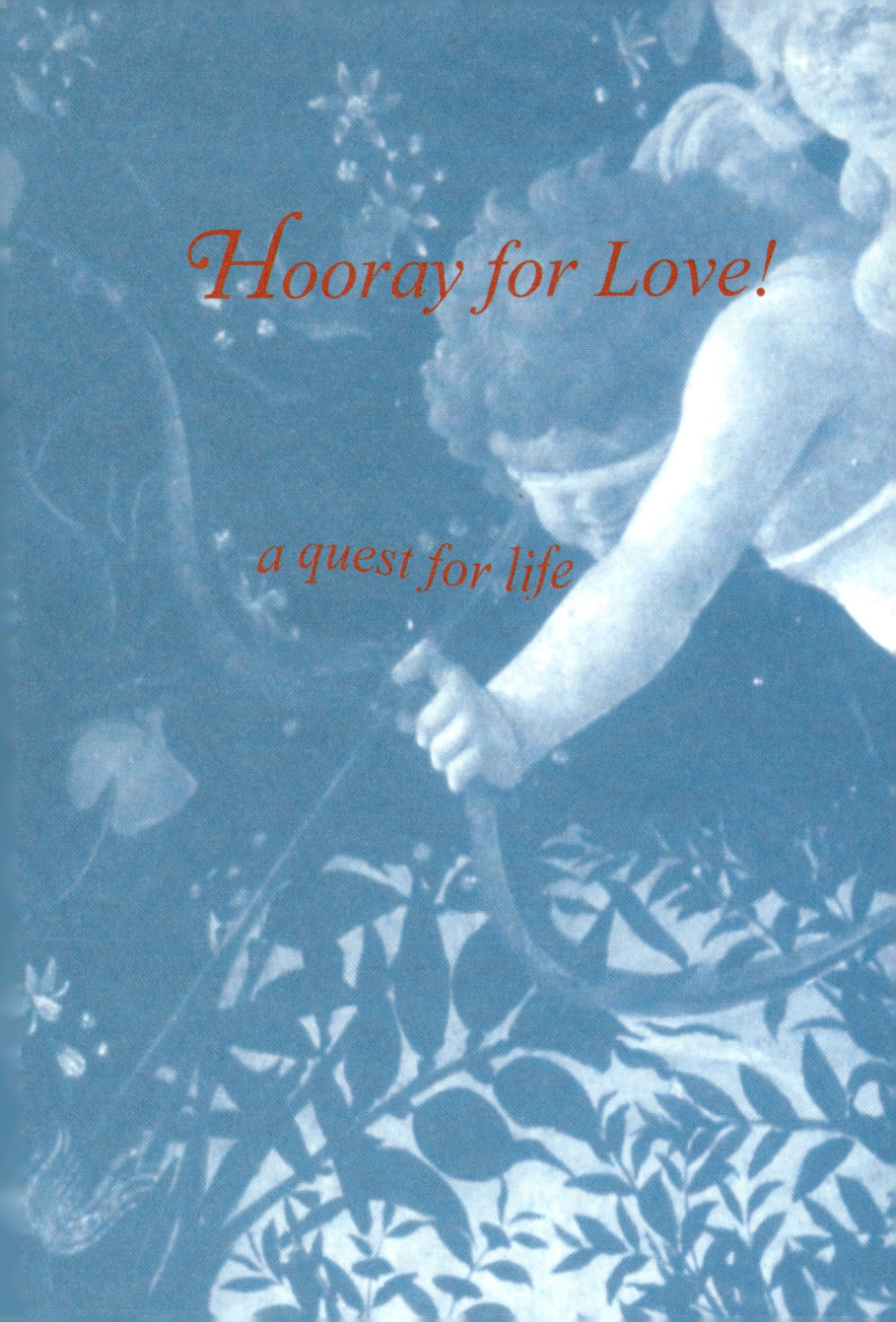

Hooray for Love!

a quest for life

Now
at the last
a grand hooray for
something worth cheering.
A personal account of early hopes,
of dashed dreams of love, and
of a search for a practical
way to give the
word, love,
life.

HOORAY

FOR LOVE

"*All* the world loves a lover!"

So they say. Yet, as with all the things that *they* say, the impertinent question keeps arising—

"Is it *true*? *Really true*?!"

The world sitting on its fanny in a dark room watching lovers flickering on the silver screen no doubt loves lovers. Yes, Valentino and Garbo and Barrymore and Gable and Marilyn and Mature. Whether they can act or not we love them. Maybe we love them even more, watching them try so hard to breathe life into a dream. But that's the movies and it's the place to dream. Now in life...

Lovers mostly have a hard time in life—and in legend. Take Sir Lancelot or Paolo or Don Juan or Romeo or Lothario, a few of our more famous mundane lovers. Then there are the stupendous spiritual lovers like Savonarola and Joan and Hallaj and Jesus and Zarathustra. They really had it hard. If all the world loves a lover, you'd think such folk would receive better treatment. And if we all loved lovers so much, you'd think we'd love love some, so there might be more love and loving and lovingness around. Wouldn't you?

When you open your eyes and take a scan around the world you'll be hard pressed to find much love. Watch how children treat each other in schools. Walk the "mean" streets, go to town board meetings, ride the subway, speed the freeways, listen to loving couples shouting in their houses. Or if all you have is television, click on the news—the same everyday mayhem mushroomed to horrific proportions—beatings and murders and serial killers and riots and war. Not much love. Despite songs about it and intense dramas about it and repeated expressions of it. "I love you, I love you." Some of us can't even get off the phone without warbling those little words.

Somebody once said if there's counterfeit there must be real coin somewhere. So there must be real love somewhere. Real love must be possible somewhere. And perhaps it's even possible here, in this nasty world we've made.

Holding to this tiny curl of hope I should like to propose that love is the only thing of value in the whole wide universe, and that loving is the only thing worth doing. Furthermore, I submit that the earth is the place for love. (Robert Frost said that, too.) Frankly speaking, it is the only action perfectly suited to a human being.

As for myself, I've been in love with the idea of love for a long time. Since I was a kid. And when you dwell on something for a long time, good or bad, eventually there's an outcome. You draw something to you or you fall into something.

Where my ruminations and preoccupation with dreams of love led me was to Master William Shakespeare.

Archaic and passé as he may perchance seem in a hip, slick and soul-rapping world, Willie-the-Shake can open the door to understanding a host of important things. Love being one of them. He wrote a play, which everybody knows, called *Romeo and Juliet*. In it the hero himself is in love with love. I had a rendezvous with this play.

I was a callow kid in college at the time. It was spring as I remember and the "Theah-tuh" Department was trumpeting out the call. Actors were needed for its full-scale production of *Romeo and Juliet*. As it was spring and as the sky was blue and the fragrance of women was everywhere, I didn't want to get involved in a play—with all those lines to memorize and all those rehearsals in a dank, empty theater. No, it was spring and I was—I must've been—worshipping at the altar of some goddess or other and I—I—

I—I needed time to suffer! True, I had done some acting, and I thought I was pretty good at it, too. My most recent triumph had been my portrayal of Tiresias, the blind prophet in *Oedipus Rex*.

But I never liked cattle calls. If they wanted me let them call me was my approach. Plus, it was spring! I was a proud, rebellious, pimply, skinny kid at the time, with about the same concentration of skinniness I have now. The only loss over time has been the loss of the weight of my precious hair.

But you can't fight destiny. I didn't want to get in a play and I didn't want to try out for Romeo (in fact it was the last part I wanted to play). I wanted to be free in the springtime for once, but I happened to be walking by the building where they were holding auditions. And, God knows, I had to be passing somewhere.

Just at that moment Steve Greenberg—he who was to become my best friend in the whole world—happened to stick his head out the door.

"Why don't you come in and try out, Frank?"

"Nah."

"Come on and try out."

"I got too much to do," I grumbled unconvincingly.

"Come on, Frank. You're good."

"Yeah, I know."

Things remained at a stalemate until a girl appeared. I knew her vaguely, and she knew me even more vaguely, but she murmured, "You got nothing to lose by trying out, Frankie."

Sure, I thought, nothing to lose except my pride. Suppose I get turned down. Suppose I read with all my heart and I don't get the part. I got something to lose. But perhaps it was the way she said "Frankie" or the way she smiled that hooked me, for I changed my mind and succumbed to the will of the stars. I went in, and mounted the stage.

Prayer doesn't always get you what you want but it always gets you something. So I prayed fervently through the try-outs: I don't want to play Romeo, Lord. Please, don't give me Romeo. I hate Romeo, Lord. Please don't let the director pick me for the part. I felt justified in praying this prayer because I had done some directing and I would never cast me as Romeo. Nobody in their right mind would cast me as Romeo—unless they were blind or blind drunk. Not with a face like mine. Not with the harsh and slicing edges I have to my character. No, nobody would cast me. Right, Lord?

And sure enough...

Things have a way of working out just right. I gave a decent reading (which satisfied my pride) but I didn't get the part. I went through the mill and did it stalwartly (which made me feel like a man) but God and his Universe of Lawful Endeavor would not allow me to play Romeo (which was an attestation to His Perfection).

All of this emotional minestrone hinged upon a funny, fuzzy guy named Wilson Lehr, long since dead, God rest his flexible soul. He tried, I do admit that. He tried to cast me as Romeo. He wanted me to play Romeo, very badly. He didn't want a stereotyped handsomeness, he explained. So he kept me reading first with this broad and then that one, all the while injecting little jujubes of direction, asking me to try this—try to be more sugary—or—not so metallic—or—as if you're petting a mink coat, etcetera, etcetera— trying hard to squeeze me into the part. Trying not to let him down, I kept trying. But, you know, I didn't really believe in Romeo.

So, eventually Wilson cast a very classically handsome, very well-built, amazingly untalented fellow named Burt Waldbaum as Romeo. (Burt, by the way, became a cult leader down in Florida, where he teaches people not to eat animals and be "vegans" or somesuch.) Burt got the role, and of course, he got the girl, but I got the play, because I got the part of Mercutio.

Mercutio is one in a million. He is one of the great stage characters, he's an actor's dream.

FOR LOVE

While *Romeo and Juliet* embodies one of the world's great love tales—sweet, lyrical, tragic—it also happens to contain a character who is more alive than most breathing beings: Mercutio. When Mercutio appears, he lights up the stage; and the audience is always waiting and hoping for him to re-appear.

Mercutio's flamboyant presence so captivates us, he takes the focus of the play. We are interested in the fate of the star-crossed lovers, beautiful and handsome as they are, but we long to see Mercutio. He dazzles us. We never know what he is going to say or do nor with what verve and imagination he will do it. He inspires us whenever he enters a scene. And we miss him when he's offstage, especially when other characters, with speeches long as their beards, drone shakespeareanly on. Mercutio embodies what we all wish we possessed. He thinks fast, is poetic, witty, truthful, imaginative, spontaneous, free, lively, full of joy. His name derives from Mercury, the fleet-footed messenger god. Mercurial, like the liquid silver in the thermometer—quicksilver.

So I got the role of Mercutio. The opportunity of a lifetime, in what promised to be a dazzler of a show. And as the rehearsal rolled on, it more and more kept its promise. A flexible, ingenious set, sumptuous costumes, evocative lighting and a very decent cast with honey-haired Mimi Strongin as Burt's co-star. And—what ho!—Verona, an old Italian town, sprang to life on the stage with all the moonlight and lyricism, the clashing families, the fighting, shouting and thumb-biting on the streets. What a drama!

But there was another drama I was involved in, a drama within a drama. This can happen in a play: an actor or actress can attract elements from real life that parallel the tribulations of the very character they're playing. Like actor Pat Hingle, playing Job, the much-afflicted Biblical figure, who wound up stepping into an empty elevator shaft. Like Mercutio, I found myself up against

FOR LOVE

the dull and exasperating forces of a world that wanted to quench my flame.

Here's how it went: as the rehearsals got going the advertising got going, too, and press releases and pictures and advertisements went out but there's never mention of the fellow playing Mercutio. No one seems to know why.

There are repeated apologies and promises that this week's releases will be different. Yet, each time, many actors are mentioned, minor ones, but no mention of me.

I thought that since I was really starting to become the part, it would be strategic to mention my name, a perfectly fine Italian name. And I wasn't the only Italian in the production; a guy named Tony played Juliet's father. In my naiveté I thought all the world appreciated an Italian with talent.

Like the character I played, I drew envious looks. So, despite remorse and more promises, nothing changed. Nothing at all.

I was, like Mercutio, in the grip of *la forza del destino*, and like him, I raged vainly.

My family and my friends ask me why I'm not mentioned. I shrug my shoulders. No one knows I'm in the play! Until the performance. And then the reviews.

Then everybody knew I was in it. I couldn't walk on campus without someone shouting across the quad to me, and when months later, at graduation, I bounded up to get the poetry prize Mrs. Doppler's eyes lit up and she greeted me, squealing—"M-e-r-c-u-t-i-o!"

Though my college career ended triumphantly, Mercutio's end was far from it. His is a tragic end. A tragedy within a tragedy. When his end comes it comes quickly, unexpectedly. He and his crony Benvolio—who, by the way, was in charge of the advertising—are striding along the street when they meet the villain Tybalt, a member of Juliet's family, a vicious character—played by Alex Wipft—Alex Wi-p-f-t—how I remember that name! Tybalt is a slimy, pretentious snake, always coiling for trouble. He represents all that Mercutio loathes. As soon as they meet we know something bad is going to happen. Love won't show its face on this street corner. First the words fly and then the swords flash. A splendid sword fight. Enter Romeo, out of the blue. The beautiful Burt Waldbaum, my friend, acting as keeper of the peace, gets between Mercutio and Tybalt, and before I know it a sword slides between my ribs. The snake has struck under Romeo's arm.

Then comes Mercutio's final scene. Held in the arms of his friends, as he breathes his last and knows it, he puns, and puns bitterly.

Romeo—Courage, man. The hurt cannot be much.

Mercutio—No, 'tis not so deep as a well, nor so wide as a church door; but 'tis enough, 'twill serve. Ask for me tomorrow, and you shall find me a grave man.

This scene was easy for me, because I had

been practicing dying on the streets of Brooklyn for years. Dying was the best part of any part. We'd vie for a chance to die. Any way would do: blasted by a six-gun, impaled by a spear, shafted by an arrow, punctured by a poison dart or stabbed by a sword.

Swords were my favorite. So, fate put me on the big stage in Gershwin Hall at Brooklyn College, dying, in of all things, a love play. Mercutio dies, as we all must. And they carry him off.

That happens at the beginning of Act III. The play has a long way to go, and some people feel that the play is over. It does feel that way. Time moves slowly for the audience as the tragedy unravels and, with some relief, finally ends for the two beautiful, star-crossed lovers.

Events, real or imaginary, turn the wheels of philosophy. And I, moved by my contact with William Shakespeare, began to wonder about love and about tragedy and how they seem to

FOR LOVE

stroll down the lane together. But why, I asked myself, why is it so?

Here in a world hungry for love, everybody drawn to it, everybody wishing for it, why is it that the world is so rife with tragedy? Wherever I turned I saw it—in my family, with my friendships, in my own petty romances. They start out with such high hopes. Then, as the slogan goes in *The Glass Menagerie*—Things have a way of turning out so badly.

If you worry a question long and persistently enough, sometimes you get yourself an answer. So, I worried my question. I was so eaten up by it I nearly entered a monastery. Why do things end up the way they do; and why don't they turn out the way they should?

At bottom are lies and twisted ideas and misunderstandings and negative emotions like hatred and envy and greed and just plain nastiness. But why do these things dominate our lives? Why? I couldn't see how things could be any different.

In me, of course, and in everybody else. And I would have gone around in the same circle unless I had come in touch with a whole new way of looking at life and a whole new way of living life.

So as luck or whoever rules the stars would have it my new-found friend, Steve, had a father, and it was he, dear Milton Greenberg, that unstinting giver of good things, who steered me in a true direction.

"Gurdjieff is the man you are looking for," Milton announced fervently, at one of our midnight conversations. My heart stirred with joy. I sensed I was about to find the answer to all my burning questions.

The breath of new life—historically—comes out of the East, and this is where George Gurdjieff arose. He came to the West in the early days of the last century. He came to America; he came to New York (where Milton saw him); he even came to Coney Island.

And he brought with him a new teaching.

FOR LOVE

A teaching that's all about love and how to make it real; that's all about the triumph of love, in our dark and naughty world.

HOORAY

FOR LOVE

Yes, the sun rises in the East and so does the new light for each dark age. This is how it has been in the past: Zoroaster, Buddha, Moses, Jesus, Muhammad and more recently Rumi and The Bab and Baha'ullah. They all arose in the East.

So there must be a law about this as there is about everything else. The new light that each one brings flares like a match struck at the end of a dark alley—or a dark age. As if the hand of darkness can't help itself and has to flick on the light.

HOORAY

A dark age never knows it is dark, not having light to make the contrast. A dark age lives in a dark dream that it is an enlightened time. This is what makes its darkness so deep. Look at our enlightened times: a canned and soda-pop society foisting its "culture" on the world—and gaining countless devotees. Destruction is called development. Noise is labeled music. Mastering trivia is the height of education.

Into this our darkness a light has shone. A peculiar, unpredictable light. Not every sun that also rises sports such dashing moustachios. This sun comes from a corner of the world where a moustache is not the insignia of a villain.

Born within spitting distance of Mt. Ararat, where Noah's Ark supposedly ran aground, of an Armenian mother and Greek father, self-taught, self-willed, unvictimized by higher education, a seeker and a finder, this self-styled herald of a new world carried with him an old-time smell that blended with a thoroughly modern mentality.

FOR LOVE

What makes the advent of George Gurdjieff so right as light-bringer to these chaotic times is that he doesn't fit the stereotype of seer or sage. He doesn't wear sandals or a robe or smile a sanctimonious smile. He wears pants, eats with a knife and fork. He listens attentively; he speaks precisely. He is kind, tender; he shouts and curses. He works. He's a man to be reckoned with. He destroys any dream we may be spinning about making him into a guru.

The teaching that Gurdjieff brought and taught is so radically different than any other Eastern import it has been called an "unknown teaching." Starting with a shockingly accurate description of man in his usual state, it presents an exact, practical strategy for human evolution. Its psychology shows people how to actually do something with their lives—how to get free of old mind-sets and habit-patterns—how to harmonize the mind, the emotions and the physical body.

Through exercises in observation and the

development of attention, a person can generate the force necessary to transform negative energy, to dismantle the false ego, and connect to the real "I" within. In this way, a person can go beyond the small, petty world of me-and-mine to the larger world of humanity and life on earth—and become a positive force in the great cosmic process.

As we and our box-car load of third, fourth and fifth world countries go careening into the new millennium, we'd best have a more spiritual teaching than good old galloping consumption to sustain us—and bring us together.

And it had better be free of priests and bible-bangers and dogmatism and gullible believers.

And it had better be something people can live in the circumstances of their own lives, every day of the week.

And it had better be true and unadorned.

And it had better be a real teaching that people can work at and not a musty old dream-teaching.

Though this teaching is tailor-made for the world we've made, it doesn't go down easy. For those who prefer not to look at the way things really are it can be irritatingly offensive. Take Gurdjieff's assessment of the lives we lead, the springboard for his whole teaching:

We—meaning me, or you, or whoever is reading these words—are sleeping, asleep on our feet, dreaming our lives away. All our thoughts, plans, efforts and reactions come out of this walking-sleeping-dreamy state. The real world is all around us but we are out of touch with it.

Nourished by our families and friends, by the society we swim in—with all its current ideas and institutions—the sleep enters every stratum, drifting like chloroform, permeating our media, our religion, our politics, our arts.

This sleep of our is an hypnotic sleep, and all-pervading. It is so deep we imagine that we are awake and that we are acting as conscious beings, oblivious of the clanking fact that all we think, do and say issues from a personal, subjective fantasy world. We live in sleep and we die in sleep.

Hardly a message to gain thousands of blissed-out-sappy-happy disciples. Or to get Gurdjieff the messenger recognition in the Encyclopedia Britannica: it's taken the Eeebee three-quarters of a century to begrudgingly squeeze out two small paragraphs on him.

Undaunted by the lack of popular acclaim, Mr. Gurdjieff goes on delineating the place of self-deception and imagination in our usual state of waking-walking-sleep. In it, he says, we are able to deceive ourselves *about* ourselves continually, weaving dream pictures and dream stories around our exaggerated self-importance, and growing troubled and offended and distressed only when life and others defy the fantasy.

Our imagination, which could—if we were in a real waking state—be used to create, is devoted to puffing ourselves up. We imagine, and we believe the spinnings of our imagination.

Unconscious, we imagine we are conscious; subjective and touchy, we imagine we are objective; ignorant, we imagine we know; unable to fix our own life, we correct everyone else's; a whole, contradictory and unruly crowd, we imagine that we are one single, integrated person (explaining away the myriad of brawling selves within us as "the many sides of a rich and varied character").

Furthermore, driven by passing desires and moods, we believe ourselves to be possessors of will, and of "will-power," as well as of freedom of choice.

And to top it off, possessing neither stability nor substance, we imagine and believe that we are *immortal*.

This delightful dream picture so completely satisfies us that we never make any actual effort to earn these precious capacities.

Enough, enough, you say. Why dwell on all this rigamarole about sleep anyway, even if it is true? If it's true we're going to forget it anyway and go on dreaming, what's the point? And what the hell does all this have to do with love?

Well, one reason I bring it up, in such a sweetie-pie pudding of a book on love, is that it may shed some light on the collegiate quandary I mentioned earlier. (You remember—why is there so little love around when we sing about it and wish for it so much?) If people are not really awake and are just sleepwalking—acting and talking from their dreams—how can they be expected to love? If each is sleeping and dreaming their own dream how can they see one another and listen to one another? Doesn't all the hurt and harm and killing we do happen because we're not in touch with the real world?

If we could rouse ourselves from this sleep that Gurdjieff's teaching alerts us to, we could begin on the path of love. We could learn how to love and we could develop the ability to love.

In contrast to most New Age fluff, "love" is downplayed in the Teaching, so much so that some assume it to be a loveless system. But any teaching—just like a bowling ball—can be given a spin. Everything depends on emphasis.

Though Gurdjieff's message is often delivered in a chilly fashion, it can be presented far more warmly—and truthfully. It can provide us with a practical way to love and magnify that love throughout a hungering universe.

To taste the true flavor of his teaching all we need do is look at the man himself. No one who got near Gurdjieff ever characterized him as cold. And while it is true he didn't wear his heart on his sleeve, it was in the right place.

Then consider what he did—in hot pursuit of truth for 20 years—traveling to far-flung temples and inaccessible monasteries—through harsh and dangerous corners of the world—synthesizing the results—setting up schools from Moscow to Paris—spreading his message despite revolution, bullet wounds, lack of funds, dense and uncooperative students, a hostile press, Nazi occupation, car crashes and bodily deterioration—he was a man with hot coals in his pockets!

And should you hear the recorded voice of Monsieur Gurdjieff you'll be surprised at the warmth, the love, that comes across.

Then there is his much-neglected exhortation:

Make Love Your Aim,
and then
Look for Direction.

A simple sentence that holds the key to understanding the ultimate purpose of the magnificent edifice he called "The System."

When we make love our aim, neither mere philosophical definitions nor the show and surface of love satisfy us. We are willing to look at the obstacles to love in us, and work to overcome them. And most importantly, since a person, absent—dozing in the land of oblivion—can love only in his dreams, we strive to wake up and love.

FOR LOVE

Listen to the best-selling poet in America, Jalalu'ddin Rumi, a 13th Century Persian, dinning our ears with the same urgency to awaken:

> He has the work who has become
> desirous of good
> and for that work's sake
> is not identified with
> any other work.
> The rest are like children
> playing these few days
> till the departure at nightfall.
> When any drowsy one awakens and springs up,
> him, the nurse Imagination
> beguiles, saying,
> 'Go to sleep my darling, for I will not
> let anyone disturb thy slumber.'
> But you (if you are wise)
> will tear up your slumber by the roots
> like the thirsty man
> who heard the sound of running water.

HOORAY

FOR LOVE

To put it mildly, most "love" is the purest bologna. And it's bologna because it's empty and fake and without nutrition—words, mere words, as hollow as hallmarks. Words of love sound nice, sometimes. When they're set to pretty melodies. Words in place of reality—keeping the great snooze-box of the world humming happily along. But if there's anybody out there really reading this and not just dream-reading, really wanting the real thing and not the common New-Age-velveteen-claptrap about "luhv," then read on—because here comes the payoff.

If you want to love then you've got to aim for it. Love doesn't just happen. It doesn't descend out of the skies on Sundays or any other day of the week. And it doesn't come and go, not the love we're talking about. How can we expect to achieve anything without aiming at it? Who expects to hit a target without aiming? When all is said and done isn't it the taking aim that creates the target?

The catch, of course, is that you have to know what you're aiming at. What is this target that is so elusive, so ubiquitous, so attractive, so difficult to hit?

Once, a few years ago, I asked a roomful of people to define love, hoping against hope to encompass it. They said things like:

- Love is a giving and a sharing.
- Love is a connectedness, and a communing.
- Love is communication.
- Love is open, accepting, non-judgmental.
- Love is strong and tender and warm.

- When love is there life is lifted up into a realm that transcends the ordinary.
- Where love is, new possibilities emerge; the very circumstances of life are perceived in a different way.
- Love gives meaning to life.
- Love makes everything possible.
- Love is all you need.
- Wherever love exists we feel safe, nurtured and ourselves.
- Love charges our whole being.
- Peace and blessings and happiness are the result of love.
- It is the ground and sky and air of paradise.
- Love is an ultimate union.

Yes, yes, amen and yes—sweet, sensitive words all. Who could take issue with any of them?

Yet, the definitions, the poetry, the drama of love does not add up to love. These sentimental descriptions of love only serve to get us into the ballpark of love.

But how do we get out of the grandstands and onto the playing field?

Bad things come in threes but so do good. Here then are three goods—the three pillars of love. By applying these three principles to any situation in life, love can enter, love can emerge, love can permeate.

The first pillar requires that we pull ourselves together and come into the place and the moment to—actually—be there. A tall order, admittedly. Nonetheless, if we *wish* strong enough and *work* hard enough we can free the mind from the grip of the past and the future and the myriad leeches tugging at it. We come to our senses, connecting to the real world, actualizing our existence on this earth in this very right now. By doing so, our hearts can open to whatever is before us.

The first pillar is presence.

When the roll call comes and our name is sounded, we readily answer "present," though we are rarely truly present. Knowing that our bodies happen to be in a certain place hardly constitutes presence. To be present, *all* of us—heart, mind and body—must be there. Presence demands an active, inner effort. Outer events can't bring us to presence; only we ourselves can do it. What's more, we cannot bring ourselves to it once and for all. We have to keep bringing ourselves back to it till we can sustain a continuum of being there. To be and to continue to be.

If the truth be told we are mostly absent. Jarring outer events arouse us sometimes—an accident, a setback, or even someone shouting our name—but only for a moment. For the most part, we spend our "waking" hours lolling in the land of dreams.

Life in all its kaleidoscopic glory swirls around us moment after moment, yet we go on plodding and plotting, oblivious to it all.

Dreaming, dreaming of yesterday—and tomorrow.

The cultivation of presence is a science and

skill as high as any. Like any science it can be learned and like any skill it can be practiced. Alas, our educational systems provide us with neither teachers to instruct us nor coaches to keep us practicing.

Instead of living in a state of expansive, sparkling alertness we are preoccupied.

We drift.

How is a person that's absent able to love?

Once we know that we are, where we are, and who we are, we can utilize the second pillar of love.

This is the much-publicized and rarely utilized *power of attention.*

We recognize the lack of attention as a disorder and easily diagnose it in our children, but the deficiency is widespread and it is a rare adult that is exempt.

Attention is the key that unlocks all human potential. Without it, nothing can be studied, learned or successfully accomplished. Attention is the greatest force we have. When we attend we mobilize all our intelligence, all our being, all our human power.

Whatever we turn our attention to becomes illuminated. Light is shed and under that light things thrive. Everything thrives. Our studies, our houses, our relationships, our plants, our dogs, our earth.

When we can't control our own attention, we are weak and suggestible, mere puppets at the mercy of every passing wind.

These two pillars, presence and attention, make possible the third—action.

Appropriate action.

This is how it works: first we step out of dreams into the real world—we come to be—in all our fullness, here and now. Being present we can see what is before us, the reality that, in a sense, is looking at us. And then, and only then, we know what to do. Instead of acting from our whims, our personal agendas or the current urge—making our usual mess—our eyes can see what is before us, and what is actually needed. By suiting our action to the needs of the situation, we act meaningfully, taking the precise and appropriate action.

Whoever is present may love, whoever can pay attention can love, and whoever takes appropriate action does love.

When these three—presence, attention and appropriate action—come together, love flows. And it doesn't matter who or what we are loving.

This is the basic dynamic of love, all the way from a dog to God. A dog knows it is loved when we are present for it and give it attention and, therefore, see that it gets water and food and a chance to run. And God knows he is loved when we are present to him and attentive to him and take the action he would take towards the beings of his creation.

Loving is a verb and it manifests in action. Take the doing away and we are left with a mighty possibility, a great almost. Actions are what connect us to the world and each other. Talk of love in place of loving is cold comfort. If we're asked who loves us we don't give the names of those who say they love us.

People, like parents, show their love by what they do. I knew my mother and father loved me by what they did for me, how they provided for me. Food was not merely bought but it was shaped into meals and spread on the table for me with consistent regularity. I was not just given clothes but they were washed and pressed and sewn for me. I was not only given a bed but the sheets were changed and cleaned and the bed was made every day. My parents never oozed a lot of sentimental words about how much they loved me. I knew it though. How could I doubt it? Their actions showed it day after day.

What I felt as a boy, and grappled with in my youth when Shakespeare and Romeo and Juliet were on my mind, I now know for certain.

Love is the be-all and end-all. There is nothing but love. We come from love and to love we shall return. For, as the scripture says so succinctly, "God is love."

Friends, we are in a deep ocean. We are, each of us, in one of those old-fashioned bathyspheres, little, round submarine-type devices, having been lowered into the great waters. Through its wee windows, we behold the surging life surrounding us. And we are afraid, for the great waters are always trying to get in to our little bathysphere of a world.

But it is the great waters of *love* that are trying to get in, to reach us. Love is calling to us to respond to the real and leave the dream bubble we are in. We are being called to become one with the great ocean of love.

Love is really something. It is the action most perfectly suited to us, human beings.

It is the path to the Source.

Make love your aim, then, and keep aiming.

· *So* ·

Hooray for presence!

Hooray for attention!

Hooray for action!

But most of all,

Hooray for love!

HOORAY

FOR LOVE

Also by Frank Crocitto

———————

A Child's Christmas In Brooklyn

Insight Is Better Than Ice Cream

New Suns Will Arise, with John Dugdale

———————

available from Candlepower
P.O. Box 787
New Paltz, NY 12561